去宠物医院

Going to the Vet

[美]威力·布莱文斯/著　　[美]吉姆·帕约/绘

王婧/译

电子工业出版社·

Publishing House of Electronics Industry

北京·BEIJING

本书中文简体版专有出版权由Red Chair Press LLC通过CA-Link International LLC授予电子工业出版社，未经许可，不得以任何方式复制或抄袭本书的任何部分。

版权贸易合同登记号　图字：01-2022-0735

图书在版编目（CIP）数据

去宠物医院 / (美) 威力·布莱文斯 (Wiley Blevins) 著；(美) 吉姆·帕约 (Jim Paillot) 绘；王婧译. -- 北京：电子工业出版社，2023.6
（胖狗和瘦狗）
ISBN 978-7-121-44941-3

Ⅰ.①去… Ⅱ.①威… ②吉… ③王… Ⅲ.①儿童故事－图画故事－美国－现代 Ⅳ.①I712.85

中国国家版本馆CIP数据核字(2023)第077354号

责任编辑：范丽鹏
印　　刷：天津图文方嘉印刷有限公司
装　　订：天津图文方嘉印刷有限公司
出版发行：电子工业出版社
　　　　　北京市海淀区万寿路 173 信箱　邮编：100036
开　　本：787×1092　1/16　印张：26.25　字数：264 千字
版　　次：2023 年 6 月第 1 版
印　　次：2023 年 6 月第 1 次印刷
定　　价：208.00 元（全 8 册）

凡所购买电子工业出版社图书有缺损问题，请向购买书店调换。若书店售缺，请与本社发行部联系，联系及邮购电话：(010) 88254888，88258888。
质量投诉请发邮件至 zlts@phei.com.cn，盗版侵权举报请发邮件至 dbqq@phei.com.cn。
本书咨询联系方式：(010) 88254161 转 1862，fanlp@phei.com.cn。

目录

1 坚持住! 1

2 不怎么愉快的旅程 7

3 吃个腌黄瓜吧! 11

4 没门儿! 鲍勃! 18

5 坏极了, 坏透了, 简直太坏了! .. 22

6 英文原文 29

闪亮登场的主角们

克鲁德

艾克

绒球小姐

鲍勃

鲍勃弄来两个小箱子。

克鲁德和艾克不用猜也知道那是干什么用的，

不是要去鲍勃奶奶家了，就是要去宠物医院了。

"我这次绝对不会上当的。"艾克信誓旦旦地说。

克鲁德和艾克连忙往后退，可鲍勃却往两个小箱子里各扔了一块骨头。"坚持住啊！"克鲁德说。

　　"可看起来真的很好吃啊，"艾克说，"我都能想象出自己咬上一口时的感觉了！"

　　"这就是个陷阱。"克鲁德说。

　　艾克一点一点地朝着箱子蹭了过去，他闻啊闻，鼻子里全是骨头的美妙香气。

　　"别去啊。"克鲁德祈求道。

艾克还是走进了箱子里，"砰！"箱子门被关上并上了锁。

克鲁德抬起爪子捂住自己的脑袋，有点郁闷："为了一块骨头值得吗？"

艾克一边大口啃着美味的骨头，一边用力点了点头。

"好吧，哥们儿，"克鲁德说，"为了你，我就勉为其难地去一次狗狗最不想去的地方吧。"说完他低着脑袋，慢吞吞地一小步一小步蹭进了箱子里。

"啪！"箱子门瞬间被关上了。

　　鲍勃把装着克鲁德和艾克的箱子塞进了车里。事实上，艾克比克鲁德更喜欢开车去旅行。他尤其喜欢对着擦身而过的车辆汪汪叫，喜欢对着街边走过的孩子汪汪叫，喜欢对着自己尾巴的影子汪汪叫。

艾克还喜欢把自己的脑袋伸出车窗外，然后迎着风吐着舌头。可是这次旅行却不一样，因为他被关在了箱子里。为了表示自己的不满，他汪汪地叫啊，叫啊，没完没了地叫。

"拜托你能不能不要没完没了地叫了，"克鲁德说道，"我头都开始疼了。"

"宠物医院会治好你的头疼的。"艾克说完又开始继续叫。车子沿着枫树街开到了榆树街，再穿过主街，几乎把全城都绕了一遍，最后终于来到了令他们闻风丧胆的宠物医院。

艾克想要通过拼命大叫，来表达自己对鲍勃的诸多不满。然而他张开嘴巴，却只能勉强发出 "唔唔" 的声音。

克鲁德见状很是开心。

　　"咱们这就进去吧，"鲍勃说道，"宠物医生正等着我们呢。"

　　鲍勃推开了宠物医院的大门，一个发型看上去像法国贵宾犬的女士接待了他们，她指着座位说："请先找个座位坐下吧。"

　　鲍勃打开了箱子，克鲁德和艾克叽里咕噜地从里面滚了出来。他们朝四周看了看，发现唯一的空座位旁边坐着的竟然是马丁太太。绒球小姐正坐在她的大腿上，像在舔棒棒糖似的轮流舔着自己的两只爪子。

　　"呃，**好恶心**。"艾克说。

　　"呃，**真恶心**。"克鲁德说，"你觉得她在看着我们吗？"

"你们好啊，小伙子们！"马丁太太愉快地打招呼。

"她的确在看着我们。"艾克悄声说。

"你们是来打针吗？"绒球小姐问道。

"打针？"艾克高声说，"不、不、不、不不不，不是的。"

"别听她的，"克鲁德说，"我敢肯定，我们来这儿只是例行体检而已。"

"如果你一定要这么想的话。"绒球小姐说完，发出嘶嘶的嘲笑声。

　　"我来这儿是为了拍照的，"绒球小姐继续说，"宠物医院就要做明年的日历了，我是日历的一月小姐。"

　　克鲁德翻了个白眼儿，小声地嘟囔："真惨啊，感觉开年就不太吉利呢！"说完他扭过脸去。

克鲁德很快发现了橱窗里的一只乌龟，他汪汪地叫着打了声招呼。

克鲁德想叫乌龟的名字，但他不知道对方有没有名字。因为对方没有告诉他，所以克鲁德决定就叫他乌龟了。这总比叫他腌黄瓜好多了吧，虽然艾克总是想被人叫作腌黄瓜。

"快看看谁在这儿。"克鲁德说。

艾克对着乌龟挥了挥爪子，叹了口气："我现在突然特别想吃腌黄瓜。"

乌龟这时慢慢地抬起头来，然后眨了眨眼。克鲁德忽然听到乌龟发出一声咯咯的坏笑，他很确定自己没有听错。于是他连忙向四周看去，果不其然……

宠物医生站在门口，他手里拿着一根巨大无比的针管，克鲁德从来没见过这么大的针管。

没门儿！鲍勃！

4

"我的妈呀！"克鲁德说。

"哦，噢！"艾克大叫。

"克鲁德，艾克，"医生叫道，"你们是下一个。"

艾克撒腿就跑进鲍勃的椅子下面。"快点过来，小伙子们！"宠物医生叫道。艾克在下面死死地抱着椅子腿儿不撒手。

"快出来啊！"克鲁德大喊，"我可不想自己一个人进去。"

"没门儿，想都别想。"艾克说，"你先进去，然后等下告诉我什么情况，发邮件给我就好了。"

"无论生活遇到什么困难，只要身边有朋友陪伴，就不会感到难过的。"克鲁德说，"反正鲍勃总是这么说的。"

"可是这条椅子腿儿现在才是我唯一的朋友。"艾克说。

艾克舔了舔椅子，这时鲍勃蹲了下来。

"快出来，小伙子。"鲍勃说着伸手拽住了艾克。"没门儿，鲍勃！"艾克哭着大喊。

趁着鲍勃蹲在地上的功夫，克鲁德看到了自己逃跑的机会，于是他朝前门飞奔过去。

　　鲍勃一下从地上跳了起来，他及时抱住了逃跑的克鲁德，又回来拽住艾克的项圈，把他揪了出来。"快来吧，小伙子们。"鲍勃说。

　　艾克一路上还在拼命地挣扎着。

　　绒球小姐在一旁幸灾乐祸地说："好好享受吧！"

坏极了，坏透了，简直太坏了！

艾克和克鲁德一进屋，宠物医生立马关上了门，问："谁先来？"然后晃了晃手里的针管。

"真的太大了。"艾克盯着针管说。

"你先来吧，"克鲁德说，"我不介意你抢在我的前面。"

"实在太大了……"艾克絮絮叨叨。

"你快去啊，艾克，"克鲁德催促道，"我认为你应该先来。"

　　克鲁德说完一溜烟儿跑到了艾克的身后。这时，宠物医生伸手过来要抓艾克了。可没想到的是，艾克突然一下子滚到了克鲁德的身旁，紧接着他又来了一个后空翻，最后竟然落在了克鲁德的身后。

　　艾克把克鲁德推向宠物医生，悄声说："抱歉啦，哥们儿。"

宠物医生一把抱起克鲁德，砰地一下把他放在了桌子上。然后他猛地一针扎在了克鲁德毛茸茸的屁股上。

"嗷！嗷！嗷嗷嗷！"克鲁德大声地嚎叫了起来，"坏医生，坏极了，坏透了，简直太坏了！"

艾克都看傻了。宠物医生把克鲁德抱了下来，然后给了他一根骨头。接着他又抱起艾克，把他放在了桌子上。

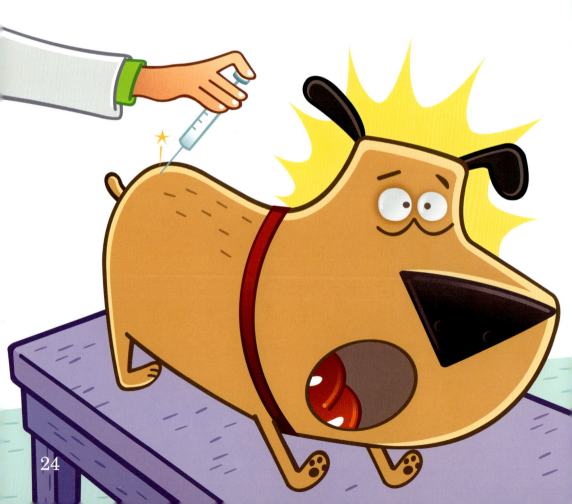

　　"真的太大了……"艾克喃喃自语。

　　宠物医生抓住了艾克的屁股。"哦，太恐怖了，"艾克呻吟道，"为什么，我刚才为什么要看到那个东西啊！"

　　克鲁德啃着他的骨头，头都懒得抬一下。"救救我，克鲁德，我这么小可不能死掉啊，我这么漂亮更不能死掉啊，而且我还这么可爱怎么可以死掉啊！还有那么多松鼠等着我去追逐，还有那么多美丽的花我都没有去嘘嘘呢，哦，真的太恐怖了！"

宠物医生咚地一下把艾克放回到了地上，然后递给他一根小小的骨头。"刚刚究竟发生了什么？"艾克疑惑道。

　　"你被打了一针。"克鲁德解释道。

　　"什么时候？"艾克问。

　　"就在你哭得像个胆小鬼的时候啊。"克鲁德说。

　　"我才没有哭呢。"艾克反驳道。他回头看了看自己的屁股，"实在太大了，"他咕哝道，"我真的不应该看的。"

　　"可是你什么感觉也没有啊，"克鲁德说，"所以，下次能不能你先来呢？"艾克摇了摇头。

　　"你是**同意**了吗？"克鲁德问。

　　"那是**'才不'**的意思。"艾克说。

　　"你确定吗？"克鲁德追问。

　　"就如同我确定跟你在一起的时光才是最好的时光一样的确定。"艾克说。

"好吧，"克鲁德说，"我们回家吧！"

两人跳进各自的箱子里，啃着美味的骨头开心地回家去了。不过，他们只能一路站着回家了！

Meet the Characters

Crud

Ick

Miss Puffy

Bob

Be Strong!

Bob set out two small crates.

Ick and Crud knew what that meant.

A trip to Grandma Bob's house.

Or, the vet!

鲍勃弄来两个小箱子。

克鲁德和艾克不用猜也知道那是干什么用的，
不是要去鲍勃奶奶家了，就是要去宠物医院了。

"我这次绝对不会上当的。"艾克信誓旦旦地说。
克鲁德和艾克连忙往后退，可鲍勃却往两个小箱子里各扔了一块骨头。"坚持住啊！"克鲁德说。

"可看起来真的很好吃啊，"艾克说，"我都能想象出自己咬上一口时的感觉了！"
"这就是个陷阱。"克鲁德说。
艾克一点一点地朝着箱子蹭了过去，他闻啊闻，鼻子里全是骨头的美妙香气。
"别去啊。"克鲁德祈求道。

2

3

"I'm not falling for that again," said Ick.

Ick and Crud backed away. Bob tossed a bone into each crate. "Be strong," said Crud.

"But it looks so tasty," said Ick. "I can almost feel the crunch."

"It's just a trick," said Crud.

Ick inched closer to the crate. He sniffed. The dog bone smell filled his nose.

"Don't do it!" begged Crud.

艾克还是走进了箱子里，"砰！"箱子门被关上并上了锁。

克鲁德抬起爪子插住自己的脑袋，有点郁闷："为了一块骨头值得吗？"

艾克一边大口啃着美味的骨头，一边用力点了点头。

"好吧，哥们儿，"克鲁德说，"为了你，我就魅为其难地去一次狗狗最不想去的地方吧。"说完他低着脑袋，慢吞吞地一小步一小步蹭进了箱子里。

But in walked Ick. Snap! The crate door slammed shut and locked.

Crud buried his head under his paws. "Was it worth it?" he asked.

Ick gnawed on his bone and shook his head up and down.

"Okay, buddy," said Crud. "For you, I'll go where no dog should ever go." Crud took slow puppy-steps into the other crate. His head hung low.

Snap! The door slammed shut.

Not a Fun Ride

Bob grabbed the crates and loaded them into his car. Ick liked car rides much more than Crud did. Ick liked to bark at the other cars, at kids walking by, and at the shadow of his tail.

不怎么愉快的旅程 2

鲍勃把装着克鲁德和艾克的箱子塞进了车里。事实上，艾克比克鲁德更喜欢开车去旅行。他尤其喜欢对着擦身而过的车辆汪汪叫，喜欢对着街边走过的孩子汪汪叫，喜欢对着自己尾巴的影子汪汪叫。

7

艾克还喜欢把自己的脑袋伸出车窗外，然后迎着风吐着舌头。可是这次旅行却不一样，因为他被关在了箱子里。为了表示自己的不满，他汪汪地叫啊，叫啊，没完没了地叫。

"拜托你能不能不要没完没了地叫了，"克鲁德说道，"我头都开始疼了。"

"宠物医院会治好你的头疼的。"艾克说完又开始继续叫。车子沿着枫树街开到了榆树街，再穿过主街，几乎把全城都绕了一遍，最后终于来到了令他们闻风丧胆的宠物医院。

8

9

Ick also liked to hang his head out the window. He liked the way his tongue flapped in the air. But not this time. Not in this crate. So he just barked and barked and barked.

"Can you please stop yapping?" asked Crud. "I have a headache now."

"The vet can take care of that," said Ick. And he kept on barking. Down Maple Street. Up Elm Street. Across Main Street. And all around the town. Until they got to the place they feared most. The vet.

Ick tried to bark to show Bob what a bad thing he had done.

But instead of a *woof*, he could barely squeak out a *woo*.

Crud liked that.

3

Eat a Pickle

"Let's get you two inside," said Bob. "The vet is waiting."

He pushed open the office door. A lady with hair like a French Poodle's greeted them. "Have a seat," she said and pointed.

　　"咱们这就进去吧，"鲍勃说道，"宠物医生正等着我们呢。"

　　鲍勃推开了宠物医院的大门，一个发型看上去像法国贵宾犬的女士接待了他们，她指着座位说："请先找个座位坐下吧。"

11

38

Bob unlatched the crates. Out tumbled Ick and Crud. They looked at the only empty seat. Beside it sat Mrs. Martin. On her lap Miss Puffy posed, licking her paws like they were lollipops.

"Oh, ick," said Ick.

"Oh, crud," said Crud. "Do you think she saw us?"

"Hello, boys," purred Miss Puffy.

"She saw us," whispered Ick.

"Are you here for your shots?" asked Miss Puffy.

"Shots?" cried Ick. "Oh, no. No, no, no, no, no-no-no-no-no."

"Don't listen to her," said Crud. "I'm sure it's just a check-up."

"Of course," said Miss Puffy and she hissed a laugh.

克鲁德很快发现了橱窗里的一只乌龟，他汪汪地叫着打了声招呼。

克鲁德想叫乌龟的名字，但他不知道对方有没有名字。因为对方没有告诉他，所以克鲁德决定就叫他乌龟了。这总比叫他腌黄瓜好多了吧，虽然艾克总是想被人叫作腌黄瓜。

"我来这儿是为了拍照的，"绒球小姐继续说，"宠物医院就要做明年的日历了，我是日历的一月小姐。"

克鲁德翻了个白眼儿，小声地嘟囔："真惨啊，感觉开年就不太吉利呢！"说完他扭过脸去。

14

15

"I'm here to get my picture taken," she said. "The vet is making his calendar for next year. I'll be January."

Crud rolled his eyes. "What a sad start to the year," he whispered. Then he looked away.

In the window Crud spotted a turtle. He barked hello.

He would have called out the turtle's name. But he didn't know if the turtle had one. The turtle never said. So, Crud called him Turtle. It was better than calling him Pickles, which is what Ick wanted to call him.

“快看看谁在这儿。”克鲁德说。

几几几几几抬起了几只手了，凹了凹气，“真想去吃腌黄瓜。”

乌龟这时慢慢地抬起头来，然后眨了眨眼。克鲁德忽然听到乌龟发出一声咕咕的坏笑，他很确定自己没有听错。了几他笑几几向四周看去，果不其然，

宠物医生站在门口，他手里拿着一根巨大无比的针管，克鲁德从来没见过这么大的针管。

16
17

"Look who's here," Crud said.

Ick lifted his paw in a wave. "Now I want to eat a pickle," he moaned.

Turtle slowly lifted his head and winked. Crud was sure he heard the little turtle giggle. As he turned around, he found out why.

The vet stood in the doorway. In his hand was the largest needle Crud had ever seen.

No Way, Bob!

4

"Yowza!" said Crud.

"Uh-oh," said Ick.

"Ick and Crud," the vet called. "You're next."

Ick darted under Bob's chair. "Come on boys," said the vet. Ick grabbed onto the chair leg.

"Come on," said Crud. "I'm not going in there alone."

"Nope. Not gonna do it," Ick said. "You go ahead and tell me about it later. Send me an email."

"Bad times are never so bad with a friend by your side" said Crud. "Or at least that's what Bob always says."

"This chair leg is my only friend now," said Ick.

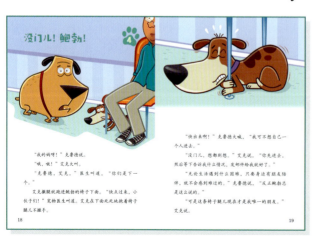

没门儿！鲍勃！

"我的妈呀！"克鲁德说。

"哦，哦！"艾克大叫。

"克鲁德，艾克，"医生叫道，"你们是下一个。"

艾克撒腿就跑进鲍勃的椅子下面。"快点过来，小伙子们！"宠物医生叫道。艾克在下面死死地抱着椅子腿儿不撒手。

18

"快出来啊！"克鲁德大喊，"我可不想自己一个人进去。"

"没门儿，想都别想。"艾克说，"你先进去，然后等下告诉我什么情况，发邮件给我就好了。"

"无论生活遇到什么困难，只要身边有朋友陪伴，就不会感到难过的。"克鲁德说，"反正鲍勃总是这么说的。"

"可是这靠椅子腿儿现在才是我唯一的朋友。"艾克说。

19

He licked the leg. Bob squatted. "Come on, boy" he said. He grabbed for Ick. "No way, Bob!" cried Ick.

With Bob on the floor, Crud saw his chance to escape. He took off for the front door.

Bob jumped to his feet and scooped him up just in time. Then Bob tugged on Ick's collar. "Come on, boy," he said.

Ick kicked his paws all the way to the big white room.

"Have fun," purred Miss Puffy.

Bad, Bad, Bad!

Once inside, the vet quickly shut the door. "Who's first?" he asked and waved the needle in his hand.

"It's just so big," said Ick, staring at the needle.

"You can go first," said Crud. "I don't mind."

"It's just so big," said Ick again.

"Go on, Ick," said Crud. "I insist."

Crud slipped behind him. The vet reached down to grab Ick. But Ick rolled on his side, did a backflip, and landed behind Crud.

Then he pushed Crud toward the vet. "Sorry, buddy," he whispered.

坏极了，坏透了，简直太坏了！

艾克和克鲁德一进屋，宠物医生立马关上了门，问："谁先来？"然后亮了亮手里的针管。

"真的太大了。"艾克盯着针管说。

"你先来吧，"克鲁德说，"我不介意你抢在我的前面。"

"实在太大了……"艾克絮絮叨叨。

"你快去啊，艾克，"克鲁德催促道，"我认为你应该先来。"

克鲁德说完一溜烟儿地跑到了艾克的身后。这时，宠物医生伸手过去要抓艾克了。可没想到的是，艾克突然一下子滚到了克鲁德的身旁，紧接着他又来了一个后空翻，最后竟然落在了克鲁德的身后。

艾克把克鲁德推向宠物医生，悄声说："抱歉啦，哥们儿。"

22   23

The vet scooped Crud up, plopped him on the table, and plunged the needle into his hairy butt.

"OWWW… WEEEE!" yelled Crud. "Bad vet! Bad, bad, bad!"

Ick froze. The vet handed Crud a bone and put him down. Then he reached for Ick and lifted him onto the table.

"It's just so big," Ick mumbled. He grabbed his butt. "Oh, the horror," Ick moaned. "Why oh why did I look?"

Crud gnawed on his bone and didn't look up. "Help me, Crud. I'm too young to die. I'm too pretty to die. I'm too cuddly to die. I have so many more squirrels to chase. And so many more flowers to pee on. Oh, the horror!"

宠物医生哗地一下把艾克放回到了地上，然后递给他一根小小的骨头。"刚刚究竟发生了什么？"艾克疑惑道。

"你被打了一针。"克鲁德解释道。

"什么时候？"艾克问。

"就在你哭得像个胆小鬼的时候啊。"克鲁德说。

"我才没有哭呢。"艾克反驳道。他回头看了看自己的屁股，"实在太大了，"他咕哝道，"我真的不应该看的。"

26

"可是你什么感觉也没有啊，"克鲁德说，"所以，下次能不能你先来呢？"艾克摇了摇头。

"你是**同意**了吗？"克鲁德问。

"那是**才不**的意思。"艾克说。

"你确定吗？"克鲁德追问。

"就如同我确定跟你在一起的时光才是最好的时光一样的确定。"艾克说。

27

The vet plopped Ick back onto the floor and handed him a small bone. "What just happened?" asked Ick.

"You got a shot," said Crud.

"When?" asked Ick.

"When you were crying like a scaredy pup," said Crud.

"I don't cry," said Ick. Then he looked back at his butt. "It was just so big," he said. "I shouldn't have looked."

"But you didn't feel a thing," said Crud. "So, will you go first next time?" Ick shook his head.

"Is that a *yes*?" asked Crud.

"That would be a *no*," said Ick.

"Are you sure?" asked Crud.

"As sure as I know that the only good day is a day with you," said Ick.

"Okay, buddy. Then let's go home," said Crud.

They both hopped into their crates and happily chewed their yummy bones all the way home. Even though neither could sit down.